I place my trust in Allah

ISBN : 9789983979114.

To the dear little Muslims 

May the peace and blessings of Allah be upon you.

You are precious in the sight of Allah, and each of you is a light in this vast world. Your faith, your love for Allah, and your attachment to Islam are priceless treasures.

Remember that Allah is always with you. Pray and talk to Allah in your moments of joy, sadness, doubt or gratitude. Prayer is a powerful way to connect with Allah and ask for His help and guidance to overcome any difficulty and find peace in your hearts.

Be respectful to your parents, teachers, elders and everyone around you. Respect is a fundamental pillar of our faith and behavior.

Be strong and courageous in your faith, and never be afraid to show who you are as Muslims. Islam is a source of pride and love, and every day is an opportunity to show the beauty of our faith through our actions and words.

Allah (ﷻ) created us and gave us: eyes to see, ears to hear, a brain to think, and a heart to feel.

It is in our hearts that our emotions are born.
Some emotions are positive like joy, gratitude and love and others are negative like sadness, jealousy and fear.

When we want to talk about our emotions, let us talk to Allah (ﷻ). Allah is always with us. He sees everything, and listens to everything, even our silent prayers.

Sometimes I feel jealous when I see someone having something that I don't have.

But, Allah (ﷻ) says that He is always just towards us.
He has granted us many things without us even asking Him.

So, true happiness does not come from having everything you want; it comes from always being grateful and finding joy in what you already have.

Allah (ﷻ) says: "If you are grateful, I will give you more."

So, I count my blessings and say, "Alhamdulillah."

When I commit a sin, I feel bad and full of regret.

Allah (ﷻ) says that He is Forgiving and Merciful.
He forgives all our mistakes when we sincerely apologize
and want to improve.

So I say " **Astaghfirullah** " and ask Allah (ﷻ) to always guide me to do good.

In my moments of fear, I remember that Allah (ﷻ)
is always with me.
He is my Supreme Protector.
He alone can calm my worries, and protect me
from all evil, visible or invisible.

So, I put all my trust in Him and I read the
last 3 surahs of the Quran.

When a friend makes fun of me, I feel anger.
But, I remember that the Prophet (ﷺ) taught us that the
strongest man is the one who controls his anger.

So I learn to be calm and patient with others and to forgive them, thus avoiding responding to evil with evil.

In my stressful situations, when I am unable to complete my tasks, I find relief and comfort in turning to Allah (ﷻ).

Allah (ﷻ) tells us that He does not burden
anyone beyond his capacity.

I believe that I can accomplish anything with the help of Allah (ﷻ).
So, I turn to Him in my prayers to give me the strength and help I
need to achieve my goals.

When I succeed in my exams or sports matches.
I feel happy and proud.

However, I remain modest and grateful to Allah (ﷻ) saying:

" وَمَا تَوْفِيقِي إِلَّا بِٱللَّهِ "

"My success comes only from Allah"

I believe that every success in my life is not the
result of my actions alone, but the result of
the guidance and help of Allah (ﷻ).
He alone grants me the opportunities, the skills and
the will to succeed.

When things don't go the way I want them to.
I feel disappointed.

But, I remember that, despite my plans, everything
happens according to the will of Allah (ﷻ), because
He alone knows what is best for us.

And that even in times of disappointment, there is often a
bigger plan and beautiful surprises waiting for us.

So, I remain optimistic, because I have faith in Allah (ﷻ) and His wisdom,
that He will give me what is best for me and at the perfect time.

When I am with my family or friends, I feel loved and well supported.

I deeply thank Allah (ﷻ) for giving me pious and caring Muslim parents, who educated me and taught me to love Allah and be a good person.

In my prayers, I ask Allah, the Most High, to reward my dear parents for raising me and to admit them to Paradise.
I always seek to honor and obey them.

Also, I thank Allah (ﷻ) for granting me wonderful friends who strengthen my faith and constantly encourage me to do good.

True friends help each other in the "DEEN" because they want to be neighbors in Paradise (Jannah)

When someone I love leaves this world to join God, it makes me deeply sad.

But what soothes my heart is that Islam teaches us that death is not a separation forever.

The day will come when we will also join God, the Most Merciful, and reunite with our dear ones and live eternally happily in Paradise.

Sometimes when I get sick, I get sad and discouraged.

But, the Prophet (ﷺ) taught us that there is good in every evil that befalls us.

It is through illness that we become stronger and more courageous, and that we learn to appreciate how precious it is to be healthy.

The Prophet (ﷺ) also said:

"وَاعْلَمْ أَنَّ النَّصْرَ مَعَ الصَّبْرِ، وَالْفَرَجَ مَعَ الْكُرْبِ، وَأَنَّ الْيُسْرَ مَعَ الْعُسْرِ."

"Know that when you are patient, you will eventually win, and relief comes after stressful times, and after difficult times, things will become easier."

Dua for healing

اللَّهُمَّ رَبَّ النَّاسِ أَذْهِبِ الْبَأْسَ، وَاشْفِ أَنْتَ الشَّافِي لَا شِفَاءَ إِلَّا شِفَاؤُكَ، شِفَاءًا لَا يُغَادِرُ سَقَمَاً

"O my God, Lord of men, make the evil go away and heal me; You are the Healer, there is no healing but Yours, a healing that leaves no evil."

So, I am patient and recite many prayers (duas) for Allah (ﷻ) to heal me, because He is the Only Healer.

There are times when I lack self-confidence.
Sometimes when I compare myself to my friends, I feel like
I'm less beautiful and my clothes don't look as nice.

But, Allah (ﷻ) tells us that He created us all in a perfect form and
endowed us with unique qualities, which makes each of us special.

So our value in the sight of Allah (ﷻ) does not depend on our appearance or our clothes. The best of us is the one who has great faith in Allah, and adopts good behavior in his actions and words.

So, I learn to love my qualities and to progress in my faith through prayer and reading the Quran.

When I can't solve exercises or understand a
lesson, I feel discouraged.

The Quran teaches us that Allah (ﷻ) is the source of all
knowledge, and it is to Him that we call upon, to help us better
understand and assimilate, by reciting this dua:

"رَّبِّ زِدْنِي عِلْمًا"
"My lord, increase my knowledge."

So, whenever I am about to study, I recite this dua.

It encourages me to do my best to
learn more and more.

Sometimes when I can't find something to do in my free time, I feel bored.

But Islam teaches us that time is precious and there is no room for boredom in the life of a Muslim.

The Prophet (ﷺ) said:
"There are two benefits that many are not aware of:
health and free time » So, every free moment is an opportunity to do
good deeds, whether it is learning, helping others,
or remembering Allah (ﷻ) (Dhikr).

So, I am learning to better utilize my time in dhikr, helping others,
learning and memorizing the Quran in order to become a "Hafidha"
and gain the love of Allah and His blessing.

My favorite activity is gardening. I find it a lot of fun!
I love planting flowers and watching them grow.

After planting the seeds and watering them, I say:
"I wish to see beautiful flowers in my garden INCHALLAH"

It is very important to say "INCHALLAH" when we wish to achieve something, because whatever we wish will come true if God wills.

When I share my things with those in need or provide help to someone, I feel great joy and deep satisfaction.

At the same time, I also feel gratitude to Allah (ﷻ) for guiding me to do good deeds and giving me the opportunity to help others.
So, I say:

اللَّهُمَّ تَقَبَّل مِنِّي

"Allahumma taqabbal minni"
"Oh Allah accept this work from me"

The Prophet (ﷺ) teaches us that every good deed counts,
no matter how small. For example, simply smiling at
someone or saying encouraging words to them is
considered charity, he says:

تَبَسُّمُكَ فِي وَجْهِ أَخِيكَ صَدَقَةٌ

".Smiling in your brother's face is an act of charity"